COME,
THOU LONG EXPECTED
JESUS

AN ADVENT TO CHRISTMAS PILGRIMAGE

ANDY LANGFORD
&
ANN LANGFORD DUNCAN

ABINGDON PRESS | NASHVILLE

Come, Thou Long Expected Jesus
An Advent to Christmas Pilgrimage
Leader Guide

978-1-7910-3579-2

Book cover description for *Come, Thou Long Expected Jesus: An Advent to Christmas Pilgrimage—Leader Guide*. Set on a green textured background with gold decorative trim, the cover features a classical nativity painting in a circular frame, showing Mary, Joseph, and others gathered around the baby Jesus. A gold banner below the image displays the subtitle, with the authors' names, Andy Langford and Ann Langford Duncan, in gold at the bottom. A gold banner at the top says *Leader Guide*.

Featured art: Jacob Oort, *The Adoration of the Shepherds* (1601–1671), oil on canvas, Museum of Fine Arts, Valenciennes, France.

CONTENTS

Come, Thou Long Expected Jesus
An Advent to Christmas Pilgrimage

Come, Thou Long Expected Jesus
978-1-7910-3577-8
978-1-7910-3578-5 *eBook*

Come, Thou Long Expected Jesus DVD
978-1-7910-3581-5

Come, Thou Long Expected Jesus Leader Guide
978-1-7910-3579-2
978-1-7910-3580-8 *eBook*

INTRODUCTION

In *Come, Thou Long Expected Jesus*, Revs. Ann Langford Duncan and Andy Langford invite readers to undertake a spiritual pilgrimage through the Advent season. The guides on this pilgrimage are figures from readings the Revised Common Lectionary appoints for the season, and the places to which these guides take us are "thin places"—places "where heaven and earth appear to touch."

In addition, Ann and Andy introduce or reintroduce readers to a Wesleyan understanding of three aspects of God's grace: prevenient, justifying, and sanctifying. They also draw on Advent and Christmas traditions, from throughout history and around the world, and art, music, and movies as resources for the journey toward Christmas, the celebration of God's Word made flesh in Jesus Christ.

This Leader Guide is intended to help you lead a group of adults from your congregation in your own Advent pilgrimage using Scripture and Ann and Andy's book as your primary resources. Here, you will find logistical pointers, Scripture readings, and study questions for planning and leading five sessions, corresponding to the five chapters of Ann and Andy's book. (Although they assign each of their chapters to a Sunday of Advent and to Christmas Day, you can use these sessions on any day of the week.)

- **Session 1: An Early Prophet: Isaiah.** This session focuses on the twin messages of judgment and grace proclaimed by the prophet Isaiah in Jerusalem in the shadow of the First Temple in the eighth century BCE and encourages participants to reclaim Advent as a countercultural season for rejecting sin and reaching out to those who are alone.

- **Session 2: Two Later Prophets: John the Baptist and John the Theologian.** This session looks to two later prophets— John the Baptist in the Jordan wilderness, and the seer John who composed Revelation on Patmos—as messengers of God's judgment and grace, and leads participants to consider these prophetic calls to perseverance in faith.

- **Session 3: The Mother of God and First Disciple: Mary**. This session focuses on the teenage girl in Nazareth who said yes to God's saving purposes and invites participants to consider her as a model of faithful obedience today.
- **Session 4: The First Witnesses: Angels, Shepherds, Simeon, and Anna**. This session highlights the Christmas story cast familiar from pageants—the angels and shepherds outside Bethlehem and Simeon and Anna in the Second Temple—and asks participants to identify ways in which they and their congregation are witnessing to Jesus.
- **Session 5: Grace Born in Bethlehem**. The concluding session reflects on the seer John's vision of the new Jerusalem and the evangelist John's proclamation of the Word made flesh and urges participants to identify ways they can and do keep Jesus Christ at the center of their Advent and Christmas celebrations.

Although this Leader Guide is written with the assumption that both leaders and participants will also be reading Ann and Andy's book, its quotations from that book and its direct references to Scripture mean leaders can also use it on its own.

Each session contains the following elements to draw from as you plan five in-person, virtual, or hybrid sessions:

- **Session Goals**
- **Biblical Foundations**. Key Scripture texts for each session from the Common English Bible.
- **Before Your Session**. Tips to help you prepare a productive session.
- **Starting Your Session**. Discussion questions intended to warm up your group for fruitful discussion.
- **Opening Prayer**. Use the prayer as written or let it suggest a prayer in your own words.

- **Book Discussion Questions**. You likely will not be able or want to use all the questions in every session, so feel free to pick and choose based on your group's interests and the Spirit's leading.
- **Closing Your Session**. Some prompts for a focused discussion or reflection.
- **Closing Prayer**. Each session suggests a Christmas carol or hymn for spiritual use as a closing prayer.

Be sure to promote this study. First, determine the time, place, and schedule. Begin the promotion in October and consider starting a week or two before Advent begins. Starting early provides more flexibility as December schedules become more crowded. To advertise the study, share the short promotional video by Ann Langford Duncan provided by this program on DVD or Amplify to attract participants. In addition, put a short promotional piece on the church website or weekly announcement bulletin. Here is one possibility:

> *Come, Thou Long Expected Jesus: An Advent to Christmas Pilgrimage* is a short but fascinating Bible study. Together, we will read Scripture, visit many holy sites, meet many saints, and delve into the history and celebrations of these holy days. Join us at [location, day, and time]. You may also join the class through our digital platform. Copies of the devotional book will be available. Put Christ at the center of Christmas! Join us!

Also, for each session, create a welcoming atmosphere. Hospitality is a spiritual discipline. Make everyone feel welcome and help every participant experience the freedom to ask questions and express opinions. Offer light refreshments, such as Christmas cookies, hot chocolate, tea, and coffee.

Thank you for your willingness to lead! May you and your group find your pilgrimage toward Christ's birth this year invigorating, inspiring, and nourishing to your faith all year long and for many Advent and Christmas seasons to come.

SESSION 1

AN EARLY PROPHET

ISAIAH

SESSION GOALS

This session's reading, reflection, discussion, and prayer will help participants:

- reflect on the nature and significance of pilgrimages, both actual pilgrimages and our pilgrimage through life;
- consider the concept of thin places and identify such places in their lives;
- understand the importance of Jerusalem and the First Temple in Jewish history and faith;
- ponder messages of judgment and hope the prophet Isaiah preached in the eighth century BCE and appreciate their importance as messianic prophecies in the Christian faith;
- define prevenient grace and identify ways in which they have experienced it; and
- reclaim Advent as a countercultural season for naming sin, rejecting secular holiday excesses, listening to prophets, and reaching out to those who are alone.

BIBLICAL FOUNDATIONS

Hear you heavens, and listen earth,
for the LORD has spoken:

I reared children; I raised them,
  and they turned against me!...

Doom! Sinful nation, people weighed down with crimes,
  evildoing offspring, corrupt children!
They have abandoned the LORD,
  despised the holy one of Israel;
  they turned their backs on God.

Isaiah 1:2, 4

In the days to come
  the mountain of the LORD's house
  will be the highest of the mountains.
  It [Jerusalem] will be lifted above the hills;
    peoples will stream to it.
Many nations will go and say,
  "Come, let's go up to the LORD's mountain,
  to the house of Jacob's God
    so that he [the LORD] may teach us his ways
    and we may walk in God's paths."...
Then they will beat their swords into iron plows
  and their spears into pruning tools.
Nation will not take up sword against nation;
  they will no longer learn how to make war.

Isaiah 2:2-4

The people walking in darkness have seen a great light.
  On those living in a pitch-dark land, light has dawned....
A child is born to us, a son is given to us,
  and authority will be on his shoulders.
  He will be named
  Wonderful Counselor, Mighty God,
  Eternal Father, Prince of Peace.
There will be vast authority and endless peace
  for David's throne and for his kingdom,
  establishing and sustaining it
  with justice and righteousness
  now and forever.

Isaiah 9:2, 6-7

BEFORE YOUR SESSION

- Carefully and prayerfully read this session's Biblical Foundations more than once. Note words and phrases that attract your attention and meditate on them. Write down questions you have and try to answer them, consulting trusted Bible commentaries.

- Carefully read the introduction and chapter 1 of *Come, Thou Long Expected Jesus* more than once.

- You will need Bibles for in-person participants or screen slides prepared with Scripture texts for sharing (identify the translation used), or both; newsprint or a markerboard and markers (for in-person sessions); paper, pens or pencils (in-person); Advent wreath, other Christmas decorations, one or more small Nativity sets, or Christmas lights (optional).

- If using the DVD or streaming video, preview the session 1 video segment. Choose the best time in your session plan for viewing it.

- *Optional*: Choose a recording of "Poor Wayfaring Stranger" (options are widely available online) to play during your session.

- *Optional*: Locate maps, pictures, or videos of the Temple Mount and illustrations of the First Temple in Jerusalem that you can display during your session.

- *Optional*: Prepare to display Gustave Doré's *Isaiah's Vision of the Destruction of Babylon* (reproduced in *Come, Thou Long Expected Jesus*), as well as other images of the prophet Isaiah, from a variety of artists, time periods, and styles.

STARTING YOUR SESSION

Welcome participants. Express why you are enthusiastic about leading this study of *Come, Thou Long Expected Jesus* by Ann Langford Duncan and Andy Langford. Invite participants to talk briefly about why they are interested in this study and what they hope to gain from it.

Point out that the subtitle of Ann and Andy's book is *An Advent to Christmas Pilgrimage*. Ask participants to define *pilgrimage*. Write responses on newsprint or markerboard. Lead the group in comparing and contrasting their responses to Ann and Andy's definition: "A pilgrimage is a journey with fellow pilgrims to a new place in search of an expanded understanding about one's own self, others, and God."

Discuss:

- How, if at all, is a pilgrimage different from a journey or a trip?
- If you could go on a pilgrimage anywhere, where would you go? With whom? Why?
- Ann and her mother completed a week-long pilgrimage on one part of the Camino de Santiago (the Way of St. James) from Portugal to Spain. Have you or has someone you know taken a pilgrimage? Where? Why?
- As Ann and Andy note, Joseph Campbell, the famous scholar of world mythology, "describes pilgrimages as a kind of hero's quest, which is the core story arc of Western culture." What pilgrimages can you think of from myth, literature, movies and TV, music, or other cultural sources? What do you think accounts for the prevalence of pilgrimage as a motif in the world's stories?
- What pilgrimages can you think of in the Bible? (If needed, prompt participants by mentioning Abraham and Sarah's journey to the Promised Land, the Exodus, or Jesus calling disciples to follow him.)
- Ann and Andy quote author Luc Adrian: "A true pilgrimage consists of leaving everything behind. . . . But what is perhaps most difficult is leaving behind the perceptions that we have of ourselves and others." How and why do pilgrimages involve leaving these perceptions behind?
- Both Ann and Andy and Luc Adrian mention the presence of other people on a pilgrimage. Can individuals undertake true pilgrimages by themselves? Why or why not?
- What makes "pilgrimage" a frequently used metaphor for life? Do you find it a fitting image? A powerful one? Why or why not?

Optional: Play a recording of "Poor Wayfaring Stranger," the Appalachian folk song Ann and Andy reference in their introduction. Invite participants to talk briefly about what the song leads them to think and feel. You might ask:

- What does the singer long for? Do you share this longing? Why or why not?
- What do you think about the images of the singer's destination?
- When, if ever, have you most felt like a "stranger" in life?

Tell participants that in their book, Ann and Andy compare the Christian Year as a whole to a pilgrimage paralleling "the classic Christian path of salvation" and also focus on our movement through Advent to Christmas as a pilgrimage: "Advent and Christmas acutely remind us that God loves us before we ever loved God, invites us to claim new life, offers us the assurance of being children of God, and enables us to be more holy." Express your hope that your group's study will make this year's Advent and Christmas pilgrimage a meaningful one.

Optional: Light one candle in the Advent wreath before the Opening Prayer.

OPENING PRAYER

Eternal God, through the ages you have always called your people to pilgrimage. You summoned Abraham and Sarah to leave all they had known for a new home you would show them. You led the children of Israel out of slavery in Egypt to the freedom of a land flowing with milk and honey. Your Son, the long-expected Messiah, called and still calls his disciples to follow him. As we gather in this holy season, help us to hear your call in new ways and, by your Spirit, to respond ever more faithfully, for Jesus's sake. Amen.

WATCH SESSION VIDEO

Watch the session 1 video segment together. Discuss:

- Which of Ann's statements most interested, intrigued, surprised, or confused you? Why?
- What questions does this video segment raise for you?

VISITING A THIN PLACE: ANCIENT JERUSALEM AND THE FIRST TEMPLE

Tell participants that Ann and Andy help readers "visit through space and time some of the thin places in our world, places where heaven and earth appear to touch." They quote Pope Benedict XVI: "To go on pilgrimage is…to encounter God where [God] has revealed [Godself], where [God's] grace has shone with particular splendour, and produced rich fruits of conversion and holiness." Discuss:

- What are some "thin places" you have been or know of where God has revealed Godself to you or to others?
- To what extent ought we to expect or trust God to be revealed in thin places where God has been revealed before? Why?

Tell participants the first "thin place" on this Advent pilgrimage is ancient Jerusalem. Review these points in a brief mini-lecture about Jerusalem's history (*optional*: display the images you selected before your session to illustrate the points):

- In the Bronze Age (three thousand years before Jesus), nomadic shepherds occupied the site of what would be Jerusalem.
- By 1500 BCE, Canaanites lived in a small village next to the Gihon Spring.
- Around 1000 BCE, David defeated the Jebusites and established Jerusalem as the capital of the unified Israelite kingdom (2 Samuel 5:6-10). Jerusalem means "City of Peace." David brought the ark of the covenant (the wooden chest containing the Ten Commandments) into Jerusalem (2 Samuel 6).
- In 957 BCE, during the rule of David's son Solomon, the (First) Temple on Mount Zion (today, the Temple Mount) was completed (1 Kings 8).

- This temple stood until Babylonian armies destroyed it when they conquered Jerusalem in 587 BCE (2 Kings 25:8-9).
- Jerusalem has been captured and recaptured more than forty times in the last two thousand years.
- The Temple Mount is today the site of Al-Aqsa Mosque and the Dome of the Rock (completed 691 CE). The Dome of the Rock covers the Foundation Stone, which Jewish tradition holds is where "God created the world, Adam was buried, Abraham sought to sacrifice his son Isaac, and the Jewish Holy of Holies [in the temple] stood." Muslim tradition holds it is the place from which Muhammad ascended to heaven.
- The Temple Mount is also the site of the Western Wall, the only surviving portion of the Second Temple in Jerusalem (the temple in Jesus's time). (More on the Western Wall in session 4.)

Discuss:

- Why is Jerusalem important to Jewish history and faith? Why was the First Temple important?
- "The Temple provided space for prayer, music, animal sacrifices, and national gatherings." What places in society today, if any, are comparable in importance to the temple?

ISAIAH AND HIS TWO MESSAGES

Optional: Display Gustave Doré's *Isaiah's Vision of the Destruction of Babylon* and other images of Isaiah you selected before your session. Invite participants' responses to the art. Which ones most and least appeal to them and why? What details most grab their attention? How would they describe these pieces' moods?

Tell participants that Ann and Andy write that "every pilgrimage requires a guide," and introduce readers to the prophet Isaiah as the first guide on this Advent pilgrimage. Read aloud from *Come, Thou Long Expected Jesus*: "Isaiah spoke God's word to the people of Jerusalem and the Southern Kingdom of Judah for about fifty years, beginning in 742 BCE. He experienced the First Temple at its peak of beauty and influence."

Recruit a volunteer to read aloud Isaiah 1:2-4 (5-20). Discuss:

- What charges does God, through Isaiah, bring against the nation?
- What images does Isaiah use to communicate God's charges?
- Who (or what) is the audience for God's charges? Why does God publicly declare these charges?
- To what consequences do these charges lead?
- How do verses 11-17 more specifically develop God's charges against the nation? How might those worshiping at the temple have responded to Isaiah's words? What messages do these verses have for Christians worshiping God today?
- What hope do verses 18-20 hold out for the nation and its relationship to God?

Recruit a volunteer to read aloud Isaiah 2:2-5. Discuss:

- How is this passage like or unlike, or both, Isaiah 1:1-20?
- What future does Isaiah envision for Jerusalem and the Temple Mount? For the nation? For other nations?
- What connection(s) can you draw between Isaiah's vision in verses 2-4 and his exhortation to "walk by the LORD's light" in verse 5?
- How can the same prophet speak messages of judgment and hope to the same nation?

THE MESSIAH

Read aloud from *Come, Thou Long Expected Jesus*: "Isaiah is the most prominent of the Old Testament prophets because of his messianic vision. *Messiah* means 'the anointed one,' a person chosen by God for a specific purpose.... When the first Christians read Isaiah, they immediately perceived that Jesus had fulfilled Isaiah's vision; the Messiah had come."

Recruit a volunteer to read aloud Isaiah 9:1-7. Discuss:

- What reason for joy does Isaiah announce in this prophecy?
- What images does Isaiah use to communicate this joy?

- What do you think about the images of warfare Isaiah uses (plunder, warriors' boots, bloody garments)? How can such imagery celebrate the "Prince of Peace" (verse 6)?
- In the eighth century BCE, this prophecy may have celebrated the birth of a royal heir, but Christians came to read it as a prophecy of the Messiah. How does Matthew 4:12-17 connect this text to Jesus? What other connections, if any, can you make between Isaiah's words and Jesus?
- Read Isaiah 7:10-16. What sign does God, through Isaiah, promise King Ahaz? How is it a sign of hope? How does Matthew 1:20-23 connect this sign to Jesus?
- Read Isaiah 11:1-5. Why did early Christians read this prophecy also as a prophecy of the Messiah? (See also Luke 2:33; Romans 15:7-13; Revelation 22:16.) In his earthly ministry, how did Jesus demonstrate qualities associated with God's Spirit, as outlined in Isaiah's words?
- Isaiah 11:6-9 anticipates a messianic age that hasn't yet arrived. How do Christians understand this prophecy as pointing to Jesus?
- Ann and Andy write that the Messiah's arrival "as the weakest of all human beings—a child" is astounding. Why? What does the Messiah's astounding birth mean for you?

PREVENIENT GRACE

Tell participants that Ann and Andy use a distinctively, but not exclusively, Wesleyan understanding of grace in which grace meets us in three ways (if this framework is new to your group, you may want to write it on newsprint or markerboard):

- Prevenient grace: God calls us and we listen.
- Justifying grace: God embraces us and we trust.
- Sanctifying grace: God empowers us and we live faithfully.

Discuss:

- "God seeks us before we ever seek God.... Before people ever look for God, God has already been watching over us." What are some ways in which you or those you know have experienced God's prevenient grace?
- "We catch glimpses of God when we least expect it." When was a time you caught an unexpected glimpse of God? How, if at all, did you respond?
- "At significant moments in our lives . . . we often sense acutely God's presence with us." How, if at all, have you sensed God's presence at important moments in your life? When, if ever, do you think you have embodied God's presence for someone else at a significant moment in their life?

A COUNTERCULTURAL SEASON

Discuss:

- Ann and Andy understand Advent as a season with an emphasis on repentance—"a little Lent" in which we "name sin as sin," as Isaiah did. Do you and your congregation understand Advent this way? Why or why not?
- "Isaiah challenges us to examine the excesses of our secular Christmas culture." How would you describe your own or your family's relationship to secular Christmas? What about your congregation's?
- How else does "the holiday season," when viewed through the lens of Advent repentance, highlight sin in society and in our own lives? What are you and your congregation doing to "name sin as sin" in this season?
- Ann and Andy cite Martin Luther King Jr., Mother Teresa, Greta Thunberg, and Christian leaders in Africa as some examples of modern prophets. Who else would you name as a modern prophet, and why?
- Ann and Andy point out that many people feel "profoundly alone" in this season. How does Advent offer "an alternative

to our spiritual loneliness"? How do either you or your congregation, or both, reach out to those who are lonely?

- "Isaiah offers a vision of a world in which God intervenes and heals." How is your congregation communicating and living out this vision of healing and hope in your community?

CLOSING YOUR SESSION

Ann and Andy point to *A Christmas Carol* by Charles Dickens as both a "secular" and "profoundly religious" story that "illustrates prevenient grace." Ask participants to name their favorite adaptation of *A Christmas Carol*. (Be sure to mention your favorite too!) Note that, in all versions of the story, Scrooge (or the Scrooge-like character) reevaluates his life and relationships, repents of his past ways, and begins a new life.

Discuss:

- What does "honoring Christmas" look like, according to *A Christmas Carol*?
- How is Scrooge's story a story of prevenient grace?
- What is one new way you will, with the help of God's grace, "honor Christmas" this Advent season and all the year?

Challenge the participants to create their own devotional journal that includes their own understanding of Advent and Christmas or a flow chart or picture or timeline of their own Christmas memories. At which moments was God most evident? Participants can add to or revise their devotional journal throughout the study.

Before ending the session, remind participants to read chapter 2 about John the Baptist and John the Theologian before next week. Ask them to make note of questions they might have about the reading

CLOSING PRAYER

Close your session by singing (or reading aloud) together "Come, Thou Long-Expected Jesus" (Charles Wesley, 1744; *The United Methodist*

Hymnal, #196; https://hymnary.org/text/come_thou_long_expected_jesus
_born_to):

Come, thou long-expected Jesus, born to set thy people free;
from our fears and sins release us, let us find our rest in thee.
Israel's strength and consolation, hope of all the earth thou art;
dear desire of every nation, joy of every longing heart.

Born thy people to deliver, born a child and yet a King,
born to reign in us forever, now thy gracious kingdom bring.
By thine own eternal spirit rule in all our hearts alone;
by thine all sufficient merit, raise us to thy glorious throne.

SESSION 2

TWO LATER PROPHETS

JOHN THE BAPTIST AND JOHN THE THEOLOGIAN

SESSION GOALS

This session's reading, reflection, discussion, and prayer will help participants:

- reflect on ways in which Christmas comedy movies may serve a prophetic function;
- consider how John the Baptist proclaimed both judgment and hope to God's people while pointing to Jesus as the Messiah and identify ways they can point others to Jesus today;
- consider why John the Theologian, in Revelation, called churches to persevere in faith and identify ways in which Christians today struggle with and overcome "lukewarm" faith; and
- define justifying grace and reflect on their experiences of it in specific moments and throughout their lives.

BIBLICAL FOUNDATIONS

In those days John the Baptist appeared in the desert of Judea announcing, "Change your hearts and lives! Here comes the kingdom of heaven!" He was the one of whom Isaiah the prophet spoke when he said:

The voice of one shouting in the wilderness,
"Prepare the way for the Lord;
make his paths straight."

John wore clothes made of camel's hair, with a leather belt around his waist. He ate locusts and wild honey.

People from Jerusalem, throughout Judea, and all around the Jordan River came to him. As they confessed their sins, he baptized them in the Jordan River. Many Pharisees and Sadducees came to be baptized by John. He said to them, "You children of snakes! Who warned you to escape from the angry judgment that is coming soon? Produce fruit that shows you have changed your hearts and lives. And don't even think about saying to yourselves, Abraham is our father. I tell you that God is able to raise up Abraham's children from these stones. The ax is already at the root of the trees. Therefore, every tree that doesn't produce good fruit will be chopped down and tossed into the fire. I baptize with water those of you who have changed your hearts and lives. The one who is coming after me is stronger than I am. I'm not worthy to carry his sandals. He will baptize you with the Holy Spirit and with fire. The shovel he uses to sift the wheat from the husks is in his hands. He will clean out his threshing area and bring the wheat into his barn. But he will burn the husks with a fire that can't be put out."

Matthew 3:1-12

A revelation of Jesus Christ, which God gave him to show his servants what must soon take place. Christ made it known by sending it through his angel to his servant John, who bore witness to the word of God and to the witness of Jesus Christ, including all that John saw. Favored is the one who reads the words of this prophecy out loud, and favored are those who listen to it being read, and keep what is written in it, for the time is near.

Revelation 1:1-3

"Write this to the angel of the church in Laodicea:

These are the words of the Amen, the faithful and true witness, the ruler of God's creation. I know your works. You are neither cold nor hot. I wish that you were either cold or hot. So because you are lukewarm, and neither hot nor cold, I'm about to spit you out of my mouth. After all, you say, 'I'm rich, and I've grown wealthy, and I don't need a thing.' You don't realize that you are miserable, pathetic, poor, blind, and naked. My advice is that you buy gold from me that has been purified by fire so that you may be rich, and white clothing to wear so that your nakedness won't be shamefully exposed, and ointment to put on your eyes so that you may see. I correct and discipline those whom I love. So be earnest and change your hearts and lives. Look! I'm standing at the door and knocking. If any hear my voice and open the door, I will come in to be with them, and will have dinner with them, and they will have dinner with me. As for those who emerge victorious, I will allow them to sit with me on my throne, just as I emerged victorious and sat down with my Father on his throne. If you can hear, listen to what the Spirit is saying to the churches."

Revelation 3:14-22

BEFORE YOUR SESSION

- Carefully and prayerfully read this session's Biblical Foundations more than once. Note words and phrases that attract your attention and meditate on them. Write down questions you have, and try to answer them, consulting trusted Bible commentaries.

- Carefully read chapter 2 of *Come, Thou Long Expected Jesus* more than once.

- You will need either Bibles for in-person participants or screen slides prepared with Scripture texts for sharing (identify the translation used), or both; newsprint or a markerboard and markers (for in-person sessions); paper, pens or pencils (in-person); Advent wreath, other Christmas decorations, one or more small Nativity sets, or Christmas lights (optional).

- If using the DVD or streaming video, preview the session 2 video segment. Choose the best time in your session plan for viewing it.

- *Optional*: Locate maps, pictures, or videos of the Jordan River and the island of Patmos that you can display during your session.

- *Optional*: Choose a clip from a Christmas comedy movie you think both pushes us to "confront the failures in our own lives" and "offer[s] the possibility of redemption" while making us laugh. (Ann and Andy mention *National Lampoon's Christmas Vacation*, *Miracle on 34th Street* [1947], and *A Charlie Brown Christmas*.) If possible and desired, contact participants between sessions and suggest they watch the full film from which you choose a clip before you meet.

- *Optional*: Prepare to display Gustave Doré's *John the Baptist Preaching in the Wilderness* (reproduced in *Come, Thou Long Expected Jesus*), Matthias Grünewald's painting of the Crucifixion and other images of John the Baptist, and Eastern Orthodox icons and other images of John the Theologian. Choose art from a variety of artists, time periods, and styles.

- *Optional*: Gather tracing paper for each participant, (colored) pencils to share, and line drawing chrismon patterns (search online).

STARTING YOUR SESSION

Welcome participants. Lead them in brainstorming a list of their favorite Christmas comedy movies. Write responses on newsprint or markerboard.

Optional: Watch together the clip from a Christmas comedy movie you chose while planning this session.

Discuss:

- What makes the Christmas season such a rich source for comedy?

- Ann and Andy note that from ancient Greece onward, comedies tend to "depict ordinary people at their worst to elicit gentle smiles and laughter but ultimately to take us to a better place." How do some of the movies on our list do so? (If you have watched a clip together, discuss how the clip meets Ann and Andy's criterion.)

- "The best prophets may no longer be those who point fingers and preach damnation," Ann and Andy suggest, "but the comics who poke at our weaknesses and offer the possibility of redemption." Do you agree? Why or why not?

Briefly review the concept of thin places from session 1, reminding participants of the messages of judgment and hope Isaiah of Jerusalem preached. Tell them your group will listen in this session to two more biblical prophets in thin places, prophets who bookend the New Testament and who share a name: John the Baptist and John the Theologian, the author of Revelation.

Optional: Light two candles in the Advent wreath before the Opening Prayer.

OPENING PRAYER

Holy God, who is and was and is to come, your servant John the Baptist prepared your people for the Messiah, and your servant John on Patmos called your saints to persevere in faith. May we heed both their messages during and after this time of study, that we may be ready to encounter Christ whenever and wherever he comes to us, through the Spirit, not only this Advent but also throughout our lives. Amen.

WATCH SESSION VIDEO

Watch the session 2 video segment together. Discuss:

- Which of Ann's statements most interested, intrigued, surprised, or confused you? Why?
- What questions does this video segment raise for you?

JOHN THE BAPTIST AT THE JORDAN RIVER

Optional: Display images of the Jordan River you selected before your session.

Optional: Read or sing the Benedictus, the song of John's father, Zechariah, as found in the *Canticle of Zechariah* (*UMH*, 208) and *Blessed Be the God of Israel* (*UMH*, 209).

Optional: Display Gustave Doré's *John the Baptist Preaching in the Wilderness* and other images of John you selected before your session. Invite participants' responses to the art. Which ones most and least appeal to them, and why? What details most grab their attention? What does this art suggest about John and those who hear him?

Recruit three volunteers to read aloud Matthew 3:1-12, reading as the narrator, as Isaiah (verse 3b), and as John (verses 2, 7b-12). Discuss:

- John preaches in the Judean desert. What are some other Bible stories set in deserts? How might these other biblical deserts inform our understanding of John in the desert?

- John baptizes people in the Jordan River. How might the story of Israel crossing the Jordan to enter the Promised Land (Joshua 3) connect to the story of John's ministry of baptism?

- What is John's central message? What, if anything, do you think and feel when you hear the call "Repent" (verse 2, NRSVue)?

- Ann and Andy note that "due to human use and waste, the waters of the Jordan River have significantly diminished" since John's day. How does the river's subsequent history and condition underscore the importance of John's message?

- How does John's ministry fulfill the prophecy set forth in the words of his father, Zechariah, about him before his birth (read Luke 1:68-79)?

- Compare Matthew 3:3 with Isaiah 40:3-5. Why does Matthew—as do Mark (1:2-4) and Luke (3:3-6)—identify John with the voice of which Isaiah spoke?

- What is the significance of John's clothing and diet (compare 2 Kings 1:8)? "If John were with us today," write Ann and Andy, "he might live at a homeless shelter or sleep outdoors. Wearing old blue jeans, a dirty T-shirt, and grubby shoes, he would eat out of dumpsters or ask for handouts. After taking a bath in a local stream or public restroom, John might walk up and down the streets preaching with a megaphone." What do you think John would look and sound like today? Why?

- "John preached two different sermons to two different audiences." What does John preach to the Pharisees and Sadducees, respected religious leaders of their day, who come to him? What does John preach to "those of you who have changed your hearts and lives" (verse 11)? Do you think John wanted each group to overhear his sermon to the other? Do you think membership in these groups was mutually exclusive? Why or why not?

- "At times, we all need to hear John's sermon of judgment. During the holiday season, we find it quite easy to wander away from God." Do you agree with Ann and Andy's assessment? Why or why not?

- "Even as he preached judgment, John also offered a message of grace through his baptism of repentance." How is John's baptism like and unlike Christian baptism? How is John's baptism a message of grace?

- In Matthias Grünewald's painting of the Crucifixion (1512–16), the artist depicts John pointing to the crucified Jesus as the sacrificial Lamb of God. How do you and your congregation follow John's example and "point to Jesus" today? How do you or can you know whether your pointing helps others see and know him?

- Read John 1:29-34. In the Fourth Gospel, John (not called "the Baptist" there) preaches no explicit words of judgment but only testifies to Jesus. What personal testimony can and do you offer, as John did, about how you came to know Jesus?

JOHN THE THEOLOGIAN ON PATMOS

Optional: Display images of Patmos you selected before your session.

Optional: Display the icons and other images of John the Theologian you selected before your session. Invite participants' responses to the art. Which ones most and least appeal to them and why? What details most grab their attention? What does this art suggest about John?

Recruit a volunteer to read aloud Revelation 1:1-3. Discuss:

- What do you think about when you think about the Book of Revelation? What does John say is the subject of the revelation he sees?
- According to Revelation 1:9, why is John on Patmos? Where is the farthest or most unusual place you have been "because of the word of God and [your] witness about Jesus"?
- Revelation 1:9 also states John and his fellow believers are facing "hardship" and "endurance." When, if ever, have you or your congregation encountered "hardship" ("persecution" in the NRSVue) because of your faith? How has being faithful to Jesus required "endurance"? How did or do the promises of God's kingdom sustain you during such times?
- From the cave in which tradition holds John received his vision, "observers can see the sun rise in the east and set in the west.... On Patmos, John understood both the literal and figurative visions of God's light." Where is a place in which you have been especially aware of God's light?

Recruit a volunteer to read aloud Revelation 3:14-22. Discuss:

- John wrote Revelation to seven small churches in Asia Minor, each with strengths but each "in danger of falling away from Jesus Christ." What strengths and dangers does the message to the church in Laodicea identify?
- How much of a problem do you think "lukewarm" faith is among Christians today? Why? When have you, in Ann and Andy's words, "go[ne] through the motions of spiritual disciplines but lack[ed] commitment"?
- Through John, the risen Jesus tells the Laodiceans, "I correct and discipline those whom I love" (verse 19). How, if at all, do you believe Christ or God has ever corrected and disciplined you? How is divine discipline different from human discipline? How, if at all, can Christians affirm God's discipline without approving or encouraging abusive religious behaviors?

- What does the risen Jesus promise to "those who emerge victorious" (verse 21)? What does the way in which Jesus "emerged victorious" suggest about the way his followers will "emerge victorious"?
- Ann and Andy identify what Revelation calls being "lukewarm" with what Dietrich Bonhoeffer, during Hitler's rise to power, including the attempt to establish a national church, called "cheap grace"—"grace without discipleship, grace without the cross, grace without Jesus Christ, living and incarnate." How can and do we recognize and resist proclamations of "cheap grace" today?
- Read Revelation 20:11-15. What ultimate fate does John see for those who commit and those who are complicit in evils? How do you react and respond to this vision of judgment?
- As Ann and Andy note, "John concluded Revelation with a promise from God made incarnate in Jesus Christ." Read Revelation 22:16-17. How does Christ's promise offer a message of hope through God's grace?

Justifying Grace and Assurance

Review this framework of grace Ann and Andy follow in their book:

- Prevenient grace: God calls us, and we listen.
- Justifying grace: God embraces us, and we trust.
- Sanctifying grace: God empowers us, and we live faithfully.

Discuss:

- Ann and Andy write that the messages and ministries of John the Baptist and John the Theologian witness to God's justifying grace: forgiveness and assurance of "a fresh, new start as God's daughters and sons." How so?
- "Along our spiritual journeys, moments arise when God causes us to become discontent with the place we find ourselves and the

false direction in which we are traveling." When, if ever, have you experienced such a moment? How did you respond?

- Ann and Andy note that we may experience God's justifying grace not only "in a single dramatic moment" but also "over a lifetime." What are some ways you have experienced justifying grace over time?

- Ann and Andy draw attention to incongruities between the holiday season's sights and sounds and ways in which Christians can be and are complicit in evil. What about the season, if anything, makes you most aware of this gap between how we are and how God would have us be?

- What signs, celebrations, and customs of the Advent and Christmas seasons most help you stay focused on and experience God's justifying grace? Why?

- "Works of mercy and piety are an important emphasis of Advent as well as cornerstones of Christian discipleship." In what works of mercy are you and your congregation involved this Advent season? In what works of piety?

- Ann and Andy state, "We must exhibit and balance faith and good works." How do we discern when we are appropriately balancing them? How can we correct an imbalance?

CLOSING YOUR SESSION

One relatively recent tradition Ann and Andy offer as an aid for staying focused on God's justifying grace in Jesus during Advent are chrismons (Christ + monogram), or symbols of Jesus: crosses, a fish, the Chi-Rho, the alpha and omega, and others. Ask participants what symbols of Jesus (if any) are used in your congregation's worship space, at Advent and Christmas or in any season. Distribute scratch paper and invite participants to sketch a traditional symbol of Jesus, or a symbol of their own invention, that they can carry with them as an aid for prayer and meditation during their Advent pilgrimage.

Optional: Distribute tracing paper, colored pencils, and patterns, and spend time as a group drawing and coloring chrismons. If your group is especially crafty, Ann and Andy point out chrismons may also be "embroidered or crocheted or made out of wire, beads, wood, or plastic."

Remind participants to read chapter 3 about Mary before next week. Ask them to make note of questions they might have about the reading. Challenge the participants to continue working on their own journals, including their own understanding of Advent and Christmas or a flowchart or picture or timeline of their own Christmas memories. At which moments was God most evident? Participants can add to or revise their journals throughout the study.

CLOSING PRAYER

Close your session by singing (or reading aloud) together at least these three verses of "It Came upon the Midnight Clear" (Edmund H. Sears, 1849; *The United Methodist Hymnal*, 218; https://hymnary.org/text /it_came_upon_the_midnight_clear):

It came upon the midnight clear,
that glorious song of old,
from angels bending near the earth,
to touch their harps of gold:
"Peace on the earth, good will to men,
from heaven's all-gracious King."
The world in solemn stillness lay,
to hear the angels sing.

And ye, beneath life's crushing load,
whose forms are bending low,
who toil along the climbing way
with painful steps and slow,
look now! for glad and golden hours
come swiftly on the wing.
O rest beside the weary road,
and hear the angels sing!

For lo! the days are hastening on,
by prophet seen of old,
when with the ever-circling years
shall come the time foretold
when peace shall over all the earth
its ancient splendors fling,
and the whole world send back the song
which now the angels sing.

SESSION 3

THE MOTHER OF GOD AND FIRST DISCIPLE

MARY

SESSION GOALS

This session's reading, reflection, discussion, and prayer will help participants:

- reflect on what role Mary plays, if any, in their own faith and appreciate her importance to other Christians;
- understand the historical background of Sepphoris and Nazareth, where Mary lived and Jesus was raised;
- examine the story of the Annunciation as Mary's strong decision of holy obedience to God;
- attend to Mary's psalm of praise, the Magnificat, as a proclamation of God's values and priorities and consider its ethical implications; and
- consider how God continued sanctifying Mary after Jesus was born and look back on their own pilgrimages through life for signs of God's sanctifying work.

BIBLICAL FOUNDATIONS

When Elizabeth was six months pregnant, God sent the angel Gabriel to Nazareth, a city in Galilee, to a virgin who was engaged to a man named Joseph, a descendant of David's house. The virgin's name was Mary. When the angel came to her, he said, "Rejoice, favored one! The Lord is with you!" She was confused by these words and wondered what kind of greeting this might be. The angel said, "Don't be afraid, Mary. God is honoring you. Look! You will conceive and give birth to a son, and you will name him Jesus. He will be great and he will be called the Son of the Most High. The Lord God will give him the throne of David his father. He will rule over Jacob's house forever, and there will be no end to his kingdom."

Then Mary said to the angel, "How will this happen since I haven't had sexual relations with a man?"

The angel replied, "The Holy Spirit will come over you and the power of the Most High will overshadow you. Therefore, the one who is to be born will be holy. He will be called God's Son. Look, even in her old age, your relative Elizabeth has conceived a son. This woman who was labeled 'unable to conceive' is now six months pregnant. Nothing is impossible for God."

Then Mary said, "I am the Lord's servant. Let it be with me just as you have said." Then the angel left her.

Luke 1:26-38

Mary said,

"With all my heart I glorify the Lord!
    In the depths of who I am I rejoice in God my savior.
He has looked with favor on the low status of his servant.
    Look! From now on, everyone will consider me highly favored
        because the mighty one has done great things for me.
Holy is his name.
    He shows mercy to everyone,
        from one generation to the next,
        who honors him as God.
He has shown strength with his arm.
    He has scattered those with arrogant thoughts and proud inclinations.

He has pulled the powerful down from their thrones
and lifted up the lowly.
He has filled the hungry with good things
and sent the rich away empty-handed.
He has come to the aid of his servant Israel,
remembering his mercy,
just as he promised to our ancestors,
to Abraham and to Abraham's descendants forever."

Luke 1:46-55

BEFORE YOUR SESSION

- Carefully and prayerfully read this session's Biblical Foundations more than once. Note words and phrases that attract your attention and meditate on them. Write down questions you have, and try to answer them, consulting trusted Bible commentaries.

- Carefully read chapter 3 of *Come, Thou Long Expected Jesus* more than once.

- You will need either Bibles for in-person participants or screen slides prepared with Scripture texts for sharing (identify the translation used), or both; newsprint or a markerboard and markers (for in-person sessions); paper, pens or pencils (in-person); dish filled with blue beads (optional); Advent wreath, other Christmas decorations, one or more small Nativity sets, or Christmas lights (optional).

- If using the DVD or streaming video, preview the session 3 video segment. Choose the best time in your session plan for viewing it.

- *Optional*: Locate maps, pictures or videos of Nazareth, the Church of the Annunciation, and the ruins of Sepphoris that you can display during your session.

- *Optional*: Prepare to display Gustave Doré's *The Annunciation* (reproduced in *Come, Thou Long Expected Jesus*) and other images of Mary. Some specific images Ann and Andy mention include Michelangelo's Pietà, sculptures of Mary by Charles McCollough (http://www.sculpturebymccollough.com/clay-magnificat-gallery

.htm), the sculpture *Crowning* by Esther Strauss (https://www
.ncronline.org/news/controversial-statue-mary-giving-birth
-beheaded-inside-austrian-cathedral), Mary as Queen of Heaven,
and Mary as Our Lady of Guadalupe. Choose art from a variety
of artists, time periods, and styles.

- *Optional*: Choose either a recording of the song "Mary, Did You
  Know?" or musical settings of the Ave Maria and the Magnificat,
  or all of these to play during your session.
- *Optional*: If rosaries are not a part of your faith tradition, buy or
  borrow a rosary you can show participants during your session.
- *Optional*: Invite participants to bring a figure of Mary from one
  of their home Nativity sets.

STARTING YOUR SESSION

Welcome participants. Lead them in brainstorming a list of what they
think about when they think of Mary, Jesus's mother. Write responses on
newsprint or markerboard.

Optional: Display Gustave Doré's *The Annunciation* and other images
of Mary you selected before your session. Invite participants' responses to
the art. Which ones most and least appeal to them, and why? What details
most grab their attention? What does this art suggest about Mary?

Discuss:

- How much of a presence, if any, does Mary have in your faith
  tradition? In your congregation's worship? In your personal faith?
- If you could ask Mary one question, what would you ask her,
  and why? (*Optional*: You could play the recording you chose of
  "Mary, Did You Know?" at this point, as your Opening Prayer or
  as a lead-in to it.)

Tell participants that this session's Advent pilgrimage guide is Mary,
from the thin place of Nazareth. Your group will consider how Mary is a
model of faith and discipleship today.

Optional: Light three candles in the Advent wreath before the Opening
Prayer.

OPENING PRAYER

God Most High, you are faithful to your promises, and you look with favor on those who are lowly. We praise you for your servant Mary, who embraced your call to bring the Messiah into the world. May your Holy Spirit be upon and among us now as we ponder your might and mercy, that this time may make us willing, as she was willing, to be bearers of Jesus Christ. Amen.

WATCH SESSION VIDEO

Watch the session 3 video segment together. Discuss:

- Which of Ann's statements most interested, intrigued, surprised, or confused you? Why?
- What questions does this video segment raise for you?

MARY OF NAZARETH

Optional: Display the images of Nazareth, the Church of the Annunciation, and the ruins of Sepphoris you chose before your session. Discuss:

- Ann and Andy point out Nazareth is never mentioned in the Old Testament. It is only mentioned a dozen times in the New Testament and only in connection with Jesus or his mother. What does John 1:45-46 suggest about the possible status or reputation of Nazareth (at least in Nathanael's mind)?
- First-century Nazareth sat in the shadow of much larger and wealthier Sepphoris, four miles away—though never mentioned in Scripture, and today only ruins. What places today are, like Nazareth in Jesus's time, viewed as insignificant and inconsequential when compared to "more important" places nearby? What perspectives do the respective fates of Nazareth and Sepphoris offer on determining what and who is really important?

- Mary was a Nazareth teenager when she conceived Jesus. How does imagining Mary as a teenager from your community influence what you think about and feel toward Mary?

- Writing about the international mosaics at the Church of the Annunciation, Ann and Andy say, "Everyone can identify with Mary." Why do you think this is so? To what degree do you personally identify with Mary, and why?

- According to Ann and Andy, one of the Church of the Annunciation's mosaics depicts a version of Mary from Mexico. This image is known as Our Lady (or the Virgin) of Guadalupe, which relates to Mary's miraculous appearance to Juan Diego, a peasant in sixteenth-century Mexico. Mary appeared to Juan Diego as "a mestiza woman with straight dark hair" and spoke in Náhuatl, the native language of the Aztecs. Why is La Virgen such a popular and powerful image for so many Hispanic Christians?

THE ANNUNCIATION

Recruit three volunteers to read aloud Luke 1:26-38, reading as the narrator, Gabriel, and Mary. Discuss:

- What's the most surprising good news you've ever received? What were your immediate and longer-term reactions?

- What surprising good news does Mary receive? What do you think about her reaction?

- Why does Luke set this story in relation to the story of John the Baptist's birth (verses 26, 36; see 1:5-25)?

- Why is it important to know Mary has been promised in marriage to a descendant of King David (verses 27, 32-33)?

- Both Mary (verse 34) and Zechariah (1:18) responded to Gabriel's announcements with questions. Why is Zechariah rebuked and left mute while Mary is not? What do their responses teach us about faith?

- "This story is not about gynecology but theology. The miracle of the virgin birth was not *how* Mary became pregnant. The miracle was *that* Mary became pregnant." Do you agree? Why or why not?
- Ann and Andy suggest "Gabriel and the heavens stood in breathless suspense," waiting for Mary's reply. Do you think Mary's response was in doubt? Why or why not? What do you imagine might have happened had Mary refused God's call?
- "Mary agreed to let the Word of God reshape her body and her life." What are some specific ways, if any, you would say God's Word has "reshaped" you?
- Mary's response is an act of submission. What connotations does the idea of submission have for you, and why? When is submission to another's will not healthy or life-affirming? When is it? How do we discern the difference?
- How is Mary's submission "a decisive determination in favor of holy obedience"?
- "Although Mary and Gabriel are key figures" in the story of the Annunciation, note Ann and Andy, "God is the primary actor." How so?

THE MAGNIFICAT

Recruit a volunteer to read aloud Luke 1:46-55 or read it in unison as a group (be sure everyone is reading from the same translation). Discuss:

- What words or images from Mary's psalm of praise most attract your attention and why?
- For what specific reasons does Mary praise God?
- How does Mary's psalm link what she is experiencing to the history of God with God's people?
- How does Mary's psalm proclaim God's values and priorities?
- Do you think of yourself more often as "low status," "lowly," and "hungry," or "powerful" and "rich"? Why? How does our position in society affect how we hear and react to Mary's psalm?

- When and how, if at all, did Jesus's birth fulfill the expectations to which his mother gave voice in her psalm? When and how do you see the reversals in the Magnificat taking place today?
- What ethical implications does Mary's psalm have for God's people who are lowly and hungry? For those who are powerful and rich?

Optional: Play one or more musical settings of the Magnificat that you prepared before your session. Ask participants: How does hearing Mary's psalm sung rather than read affect your understanding of and reactions to it?

SANCTIFYING GRACE

Review this framework of grace Ann and Andy follow in their book:

- Prevenient grace: God calls us and we listen.
- Justifying grace: God embraces us and we trust.
- Sanctifying grace: God empowers us and we live faithfully.

Tell participants that Mary's sanctification began before she became Jesus's mother and continued after she gave birth to him. Invite volunteers to turn in their Bibles to and read aloud each of the following Scriptures (or, if you are leading a large group, form a number of small groups and assign one Scripture to each). Ask the group what we might learn from each Scripture about how God continued to sanctify Mary.

- Matthew 2:13-15 (the Holy Family escapes to Egypt)
- Luke 2:41-51 (Mary and Joseph search for the boy Jesus)
- John 2:1-11 (Jesus turns water into wine at Cana)
- Mark 3:31-35 (Jesus asks who are his true family)
- John 19:25b-27 (Jesus entrusts his mother to a disciple he loves)
- Acts 1:12-14 (Mary was a leader in the early church in Jerusalem)

Discuss:

- How does Mary's obedience to God's will illustrate the power of God's sanctifying grace?

- "One unique experience of God, such as the Annunciation, is never the final moment of a pilgrimage." What are some "mountaintop experiences" of God you can point to from your pilgrimage through life this far? How do you carry those experiences with you as you continue your journey and growth in faith?

- Ann and Andy list several "Advent acts of piety"—Bible study, prayer, worship and Holy Communion—that can help us grow closer to God and grow in holiness. Which acts of piety do you find most meaningful, at Advent or in any other season? What is an act of piety you are less familiar with that you would like to try undertaking as a response to God? How can this group support you as you do so?

- "While many of us believe that we can anticipate our life's trajectory, most often we are wrong." How true has Ann and Andy's statement held in your experience?

- "The angel Gabriel may not appear to us, but God still speaks." How do you understand the idea of God speaking today? When and how, if ever, would you say God has spoken to you? How did you respond? How do you continue to respond?

- Although being faithful to God's call was not easy for Mary, she was faithful to it. When, if ever, has faithfully responding to God's call been difficult for you? For your congregation? Do you think answering God's call necessarily involves difficulty? Why or why not?

- "No matter the challenges, however, saying yes to God also brings moments of joy and blessings far beyond any that we could have imagined." What moments like these do you imagine Mary remembered as she looked back on her pilgrimage with God? What moments like these can you remember as you look back on yours?

- What advice would you give or have you given to a young person who is questioning the trajectory God wants them to travel on their pilgrimage?

CLOSING YOUR SESSION

Optional: If participants in your group aren't familiar with rosaries, let them see and handle the rosary you obtained before your session.

Optional: Play a musical setting of the Ave Maria prayer that you selected before your session.

Read aloud the text of the Ave Maria prayer (you may find it in *Come, Thou Long Expected Jesus* or online). Tell participants this prayer is an important part of Roman Catholic and Eastern Orthodox piety and is part of the Roman Catholic tradition of praying with a rosary. Read aloud from Ann and Andy's book: "Touching the beads on a string one by one, practitioners recite prayers and chants that have been historically important in the life of the church, including the Apostles' Creed, the Lord's Prayer, and the four sets of Holy Mysteries, which mark key events in the life of Jesus."

Optional: Pass around a dish filled with blue beads (available from a local or online craft supply source), inviting each participant to take three beads. Or distribute paper and (blue) pencils, and invite participants to draw three circles, representing beads. Tell participants blue is a color long associated with Mary. Your group will not be making actual rosaries, but invite participants to associate each of their physical or drawn beads with a specific prayer:

- a prayer for someone who is facing a difficult decision, as Mary faced a difficult decision;
- a prayer for someone who is "lowly" and "hungry," as Mary was lowly and hungry; and
- a prayer for their own continuing sanctification, as God continued to make Mary holy.

Allow time for any who wish to offer one or more of their specific prayers aloud.

Remind participants to read chapter 4 about the angels, shepherds, Simeon, and Anna before next week. Ask them to make note of questions and insights they might have. Encourage everyone to continue to add to their own personal journal.

Challenge the participants to continue working on their own journals, including their own understanding of Advent and Christmas or a flow chart or picture or timeline of their own Christmas memories. At which moments was God most evident? Participants can add to or revise their journal throughout the study.

CLOSING PRAYER

Close your session by singing (or reading aloud) together at least these two verses of "Lo, How a Rose E'er Blooming" (fifteenth-century text, trans. Theodore Baker, 1894; *The United Methodist Hymnal*, #216; https://hymnary.org/text/lo_how_a_rose_eer_blooming):

Lo, how a Rose e'er blooming
from tender stem hath sprung!
Of Jesse's lineage coming,
as men of old have sung.
It came, a floweret bright,
amid the cold of winter,
When half spent was the night.

Isaiah 'twas foretold it,
the Rose I have in mind;
with Mary we behold it,
the Virgin Mother kind.
To show God's love aright,
she bore to us a Savior,
when half spent was the night.

SESSION 4

THE FIRST WITNESSES

ANGELS, SHEPHERDS, SIMEON, AND ANNA

SESSION GOALS

This session's reading, reflection, discussion, and prayer will help participants:

- share memories of Nativity scenes and Christmas pageants and ponder why they are such popular parts of Christmas celebrations;
- understand the significance of Bethlehem and its sites associated with Jesus's birth and of the Second Temple and its site in history, Scripture, and to pilgrims today;
- appreciate the importance of the angelic announcement of Jesus's birth to shepherds and ponder who God may be using as unexpected witnesses to the good news of Jesus today;
- consider how Simeon and Anna's responses to Jesus are still models for faithful witness; and
- identify specific ways in which they and their congregation are witnessing to the good news of Jesus.

BIBLICAL FOUNDATIONS

Nearby shepherds were living in the fields, guarding their sheep at night. The Lord's angel stood before them, the Lord's glory shone around them, and they were terrified.

The angel said, "Don't be afraid! Look! I bring good news to you—wonderful, joyous news for all people. Your savior is born today in David's city. He is Christ the Lord. This is a sign for you: you will find a newborn baby wrapped snugly and lying in a manger." Suddenly a great assembly of the heavenly forces was with the angel praising God. They said, "Glory to God in heaven, and on earth peace among those whom he favors."

When the angels returned to heaven, the shepherds said to each other, "Let's go right now to Bethlehem and see what's happened. Let's confirm what the Lord has revealed to us." They went quickly and found Mary and Joseph, and the baby lying in the manger. When they saw this, they reported what they had been told about this child. Everyone who heard it was amazed at what the shepherds told them. Mary committed these things to memory and considered them carefully. The shepherds returned home, glorifying and praising God for all they had heard and seen. Everything happened just as they had been told.

Luke 2:8-20

A man named Simeon was in Jerusalem. He was righteous and devout. He eagerly anticipated the restoration of Israel, and the Holy Spirit rested on him. The Holy Spirit revealed to him that he wouldn't die before he had seen the Lord's Christ. Led by the Spirit, he went into the temple area. Meanwhile, Jesus' parents brought the child to the temple so that they could do what was customary under the Law. Simeon took Jesus in his arms and praised God. He said,

> *"Now, master, let your servant go in peace according to your word,*
> *because my eyes have seen your salvation.*
> *You prepared this salvation in the presence of all peoples.*
> *It's a light for revelation to the Gentiles*
> *and a glory for your people Israel."*

His father and mother were amazed by what was said about him. Simeon blessed them and said to Mary his mother, "This boy is assigned to be the cause of the falling and rising of many in Israel and to be a sign that generates opposition so that the inner thoughts of many will be revealed. And a sword will pierce your innermost being too."

There was also a prophet, Anna the daughter of Phanuel, who belonged to the tribe of Asher. She was very old. After she married, she lived with her husband for seven years. She was now an 84-year-old widow. She never left the temple area but worshipped God with fasting and prayer night and day. She approached at that very moment and began to praise God and to speak about Jesus to everyone who was looking forward to the redemption of Jerusalem.

Luke 2:25-38

BEFORE YOUR SESSION

* Carefully and prayerfully read this session's Biblical Foundations more than once. Note words and phrases that attract your attention and meditate on them. Write down questions you have and try to answer them, consulting trusted Bible commentaries.

* Carefully read chapter 4 of *Come, Thou Long Expected Jesus* more than once.

* You will need either Bibles for in-person participants or screen slides prepared with Scripture texts for sharing (identify the translation used), or both; newsprint or a markerboard and markers (for in-person sessions); paper, pens or pencils (in-person); Advent wreath, other Christmas decorations, one or more small Nativity sets, or Christmas lights (optional).

* If using the DVD or streaming video, preview the session 4 video segment. Choose the best time in your session plan for viewing it.

* *Optional*: Locate maps, pictures or videos of Bethlehem, including the Church of the Nativity, the ruins of the Herodium, and the Western Wall, that you can display during your session.

* *Optional*: Prepare to display Gustave Doré's *The Nativity* (reproduced in *Come, Thou Long Expected Jesus*) and other Nativity scenes. Choose art from a variety of artists, time periods, and styles. You might also invite participants who set up Nativity scenes at home to take a photo of it beforehand to share during the session.

- *Optional*: Choose a scene to show from either the 2024 film or 1983 TV adaptation of *The Best Christmas Pageant Ever* by Barbara Robinson. Your clip should showcase the story's theme of how the good news of Jesus's birth is for everyone.
- *Optional*: Bring one or more Nativity sets from the church or your home and set them out. Encourage participants to bring a favorite Nativity set or a photo of a favorite Nativity set to share.
- *Optional*: Review the two canticles associated with the birth of Jesus: Gloria in Excelsis and Nunc Dimittis. Consider singing a version of these canticles during the session.

STARTING YOUR SESSION

Welcome participants.

Optional: If you asked participants to take photos of their home Nativity scenes, invite them to "show and tell" to begin your session.

Optional: Display Gustave Doré's *The Nativity* and the other images of the Nativity you selected before your session. Invite participants' responses to the art. Which ones most and least appeal to them, and why? What details most grab their attention? How, if at all, does this art inspire them to think differently about Jesus's birth?

Discuss:

- What's the most memorable or meaningful Nativity scene you've ever witnessed, and why?
- What memories, if any, do you have of participating in or watching church Christmas pageants?
- Why are Nativity scenes and Christmas pageants such common and popular parts of Christmas celebrations?

Tell participants that this session's Advent pilgrimage guides are the angels and shepherds, who celebrated Christ's birth in the thin place of Bethlehem, and Simeon and Anna, who proclaimed him Messiah in the thin place of the Second Temple in Jerusalem.

Optional: Light four candles in the Advent wreath before the Opening Prayer.

OPENING PRAYER

Loving God, you sent angels to announce the good news of the Savior's birth to shepherds in the field, and your Spirit moved Simeon and Anna to proclaim the redemption he brings. Inspire us also, we pray, to respond to you with eagerness, proclaiming Jesus in word and deed to all, and sharing with others the goodness and grace you have lavished on us in him. Amen.

WATCH SESSION VIDEO

Watch the session 4 video segment together. Discuss:

- Which of Ann's statements most interested, intrigued, surprised, or confused you? Why?
- What questions does this video segment raise for you?

THIN PLACES: BETHLEHEM, THE CHURCH OF THE NATIVITY, AND SHEPHERDS' FIELD

Optional: Display the images you chose before your session of these locations as you discuss them.

Discuss:

- Bethlehem means "house of bread." What makes this name appropriate for the place of Jesus's birth (see John 6:35)?
- As Ann and Andy point out, Bethlehem was the home of King David's great-grandparents, Boaz and Ruth. What significance do you find in the fact that Ruth, who was not an Israelite, is in David's and Jesus's family tree (Ruth 4:13-21; Matthew 1:5)?
- How does Micah 5:2-5 describe Bethlehem and the ruler who will come from it? Why did early Christians come to associate Micah's prophecy with Jesus?

47

- King Herod the Great (the Herod of the Christmas story) built the Herodium three miles southeast of Bethlehem. How is its relationship to Bethlehem like the relationship between Sepphoris and Nazareth (see session 3)? What significance, if any, do you find in the Herodium's status as a ruin today?

- The Church of the Nativity is the oldest church in the Holy Land, and the grotto within it is one of the world's oldest continuous sites of Christian worship, a pilgrimage destination for seventeen hundred years. Why have so many generations of Christians wanted to visit the place tradition holds Jesus was born?

- Why is the Door of Humility—the low, four-foot-high entrance to the Church of the Nativity—an appropriate approach to the site of Jesus's birth?

- Long before any sanctuaries or chapels stood in Shepherds' Field, the area was simply the shepherds' place of work, where they received an unexpected message from God. Have you ever received a message from God in an ordinary place where you were working? How did you respond? With whom, if anyone, did you share what you had been told?

- Ann and Andy describe the twenty-five-foot-tall concrete security wall round Bethlehem today and mention the subdued Christmas festivities in Bethlehem since 2023 due to war. What ought Christians think and do about conflict in the place where angels sang of earthly peace to celebrate Jesus's birth?

ANGELS AND SHEPHERDS

Challenge participants to name (and even sing snippets of) as many Christmas carols as they can think of that mention angels or shepherds, or both. (Your group might have fun forming two teams, "angels" and "shepherds," and giving each one minute to name or sing as many appropriate carols as they can!)

Recruit volunteers to read aloud Luke 2:8-20, taking the parts of the narrator, angels, and shepherds. Discuss:

- "The shepherds were lowly people," note Ann and Andy, "poor and uneducated, who simply performed work that needed to be done." What workers might be a modern equivalent of the Bethlehem shepherds?
- Find and read the following Scriptures: Psalm 23; 1 Samuel 17:31-37; Ezekiel 34:11-24; Isaiah 40:10-11. How can each add to your understanding of why God chose shepherds to be the first to hear the news of Jesus's birth? How do they add to your understanding of why Jesus called himself "the good shepherd" (John 10:11-14)?
- Why are the shepherds "terrified" by the appearance of the angel (verse 9)?
- Although Christian art and Christmas art often depict angels as "ethereal winged creatures," Luke describes the angelic heralds of Jesus's birth as "a great assembly of the heavenly forces" (verse 13; "a multitude of the heavenly host," NRSVue). How does such imagery, if at all, affect your understanding of and reaction to the story?
- How do the shepherds respond to what God has told them (verses 15-17, 20)? How does their response set an example for us to follow? How can we cultivate their eagerness to respond to God in ourselves and our congregation?
- Ann and Andy describe how the tradition of Las Posadas, which originated with Hispanic Roman Catholics, is a "community liturgy" in which people dressed as the Holy Family, shepherds, and magi all celebrate Christ's birth in homes together. How does your congregation seek to include those who are today's "shepherds" and outsiders in your Christmas celebrations?

THIN PLACE:
THE SECOND TEMPLE IN JERUSALEM

Optional: Display the images you chose before your session of the Temple Mount and the Western Wall as you discuss them.

Summarize for participants the history of the Second Temple: when exiles returned to Judah after the Babylonian Exile, they rebuilt the temple (completed circa 516 BCE). Herod the Great rebuilt and expanded this Second Temple (work began in 19 BCE and continued for decades; see John 2:20), making the Temple Mount the world's largest worship site at the time. The Second Temple is the temple that Jesus knew. It stood until Roman forces destroyed it in 70 CE. Today, the Temple Mount is the site of the Dome of the Rock and Al-Aqsa Mosque (see session 1), and the Islamic Religious Endowments Authority (the Waqf) administers the area. The Western Wall is all that remains of the Second Temple plaza.

Discuss:

- What motivated Herod to rebuild and expand the Second Temple?
- Why is the Western Wall such an important site in Judaism?
- How do various Jewish, Christian, and Muslim religious and political claims continue to affect the Temple Mount today?

SIMEON AND ANNA

Recruit volunteers to read aloud Luke 2:25-38, taking the roles of the narrator, Simeon, and Anna (though Luke does not quote any of her exact words, your group's Anna can read aloud some or all of verses 36-38). Discuss:

- We don't know whether Simeon had prayed that he would not die before seeing the Messiah, only that the Holy Spirit had revealed to him he would not, and that he "eagerly anticipated" the restoration of God's people Israel (verses 25-26). What, if anything, that you "eagerly anticipate" would you pray to see before your death, and why?
- Why was Simeon in the temple when Mary and Joseph brought Jesus to be presented there (verse 27)? When, if ever, do you believe the Spirit has brought you to a certain place at a certain time for a certain reason? What happened?

- "A traditional title for Simeon," state Ann and Andy, "is 'The God-Holder.'" Have you ever felt as though you were holding God when holding another person? Who and why?

- What does Simeon say about the infant Jesus in his psalm of praise (verses 29-32)? How have his words been fulfilled?

- What makes Simeon's song an appropriate one for prayer at the end of the day, as it is used in many Christian traditions?

- What does Simeon mean when he speaks to Mary of a sword piercing her "innermost being" (verse 35)? How is Jesus "a sign that generates opposition" today (verse 34)?

- Although interpreters generally assume Simeon is an old man, Luke mentions only Anna's advanced years (verse 36). What can Anna teach the church today about the value and witness of faithful older adults?

- Why is Anna in the temple when Mary, Joseph, and the infant Jesus are there? (verses 37-38)? What can her example show us about faithfulness in worship and prayer?

- Luke calls Anna a prophet. How is she like and unlike the prophets we have met so far on our Advent pilgrimage (Isaiah, John the Baptist, and John the Theologian)?

- Simeon spoke to Jesus's parents, who have already heard many messages about him. Anna spoke "to everyone who was looking forward to the redemption of Jerusalem" (verse 38). How and why is speaking to both those who know and those who do or may not know Jesus a part of faithful discipleship?

- "Simeon and Anna remind us that God answers prayers, even when the answers seem long in coming." Do you or your congregation have an experience of prayer being answered after a long time? What happened?

- "These saintly guides remind us to be attentive to the presence of God every day." What practical things do you do to practice daily attentiveness to God's presence?

Witnessing to and
Sharing the Good News

Discuss:

- "Witnessing may be defined as one pilgrim inviting another traveler to join a spiritual journey." When and how, if ever, have you invited someone else to begin or continue a journey with Jesus? What happened?

- Does your congregation receive more guests than usual during the Advent and Christmas seasons? What do you do to welcome them? How, if at all, do you connect with them after Christmas?

- How can sharing gifts with others in this season be a way to share the gospel? How do you and your congregation continue such giving throughout the year?

- Ann and Andy note that Jesus commanded his followers to "go and make disciples" (see Matthew 28:18-20). What does or should bearing witness to Jesus in this way look like? How do you and your congregation participate in this mission?

Closing Your Session

Remind participants that early in this session, your group discussed memories of Christmas pageants. Summarize *The Best Christmas Pageant Ever* by Barbara Robinson using either the information Ann and Andy provide or your own or participants' knowledge of the story, or both. (Optional: If you chose a clip from the 2024 film or 1983 TV adaptation, show it at this point in your session.) Discuss how this fictional story, like Luke's story of Jesus's birth (and many other stories in Scripture), shows God using unlikely and unexpected messengers. Ask:

- When has God sent unlikely and unexpected messengers to you and your congregation? What happened?

- Reflecting on the chaos that often accompanies Christmas pageants, Ann and Andy write, "God calls all of us to act out our parts and fill roles that are too big for us." What is a "too big" role you believe God may be calling you to fill? Why? How can this group or your congregation support you as you fill that role?

Remind participants to read chapter 5 before next week. Ask them to make note of questions they might have about the reading.

Challenge the participants to continue working on their own journals, including their own understanding of Advent and Christmas or a flow chart or picture or timeline of their own Christmas memories. At which moments was God most evident? Participants can add to or revise their journal throughout the study.

CLOSING PRAYER

Close your session by reading this pryaer aloud) together at least the first verse of "Hark! the Herald Angels Sing" (Charles Wesley, 1734; *The United Methodist Hymnal*, 240; https://hymnary.org/text/hark_the_herald_angels_sing_glory_to):

Hark! the herald angels sing,
"Glory to the newborn King;
peace on earth, and mercy mild,
God and sinners reconciled!"
Joyful, all ye nations rise,
join the triumph of the skies;
with th'angelic host proclaim,
"Christ is born in Bethlehem!"
Hark! the herald angels sing,
"Glory to the newborn King!"

SESSION 5

THE NATIVITY OF OUR LORD (CHRISTMAS)

GRACE BORN IN BETHLEHEM

SESSION GOALS

This session's reading, reflection, discussion, and prayer will help participants:

- share memories of favorite Christmas traditions;
- reflect on how John's vision of the new Jerusalem (Revelation 21–22) can encourage faith today;
- explore the Prologue to John's Gospel (1:1-18) as a "Christmas story;"
- consider their local congregation as a "thin place" between heaven and earth; and
- identify ways in which they and their congregations do and can keep Jesus Christ at the center of Christmas.

BIBLICAL FOUNDATIONS

Then I saw a new heaven and a new earth, for the former heaven and the former earth had passed away, and the sea was no more. I saw the holy city, New Jerusalem, coming down out of heaven from God, made ready as a bride beautifully dressed for her husband. I heard a loud voice from the throne say, "Look! God's dwelling is here with humankind. He will dwell with them, and they will be his peoples. God himself will be with them as their God. He will wipe away every tear from their eyes. Death will be no more. There will be no mourning, crying, or pain anymore, for the former things have passed away." Then the one seated on the throne said, "Look! I'm making all things new." He also said, "Write this down, for these words are trustworthy and true." Then he said to me, "All is done. I am the Alpha and the Omega, the beginning and the end. To the thirsty I will freely give water from the life-giving spring. Those who emerge victorious will inherit these things. I will be their God, and they will be my sons and daughters."...

I didn't see a temple in the city, because its temple is the Lord God Almighty and the Lamb. The city doesn't need the sun or the moon to shine on it, because God's glory is its light, and its lamp is the Lamb. The nations will walk by its light, and the kings of the earth will bring their glory into it. Its gates will never be shut by day, and there will be no night there. They will bring the glory and honor of the nations into it. Nothing unclean will ever enter it, nor anyone who does what is vile and deceitful, but only those who are registered in the Lamb's scroll of life.

Then the angel showed me the river of life-giving water, shining like crystal, flowing from the throne of God and the Lamb through the middle of the city's main street. On each side of the river is the tree of life, which produces twelve crops of fruit, bearing its fruit each month. The tree's leaves are for the healing of the nations. There will no longer be any curse. The throne of God and the Lamb will be in it, and his servants will worship him. They will see his face, and his name will be on their foreheads. Night will be no more. They won't need the light of a lamp or the light of the sun, for the Lord God will shine on them, and they will rule forever and always.

Revelation 21:1-7, 22-27; 22:1-5

In the beginning was the Word
  and the Word was with God
  and the Word was God.
The Word was with God in the beginning.

Everything came into being through the Word,
and without the Word
nothing came into being.
What came into being
through the Word was life,
and the life was the light for all people.
The light shines in the darkness,
and the darkness doesn't extinguish the light....

The true light that shines on all people
was coming into the world.
The light was in the world,
and the world came into being through the light,
but the world didn't recognize the light.
The light came to his own people,
and his own people didn't welcome him.
But those who did welcome him,
those who believed in his name,
he authorized to become God's children,
born not from blood
nor from human desire or passion,
but born from God.
The Word became flesh
and made his home among us.
We have seen his glory,
glory like that of a father's only son,
full of grace and truth....

From his fullness we have all received grace upon grace;
as the Law was given through Moses,
so grace and truth came into being through Jesus Christ.
No one has ever seen God.
God the only Son,
who is at the Father's side,
has made God known.

John 1:1-5, 9-14, 16-18

BEFORE YOUR SESSION

- Carefully and prayerfully read this session's Biblical Foundations more than once. Note words and phrases that attract your attention and meditate on them. Write down questions you have and try to answer them, consulting trusted Bible commentaries.
- Carefully read chapter 5 of *Come, Thou Long Expected Jesus* more than once.
- You will need either Bibles for in-person participants or screen slides prepared with Scripture texts for sharing (identify the translation used); newsprint or a markerboard and markers (for in-person sessions); paper, pens or pencils (in-person); Advent wreath, other Christmas decorations, one or more small Nativity sets, or Christmas lights (optional).
- If using the DVD or streaming video, preview the session 5 video segment. Choose the best time in your session plan for viewing it.
- *Optional*: Prepare to display Pieter Bruegel the Elder's *The Census at Bethlehem* (1566) and the incipit (the opening words) of the Gospel of John in the Book of Kells.
- *Optional*: Bring a Nativity set from church or home and place it beside the Advent wreath.

STARTING YOUR SESSION

Welcome participants. Discuss one or more of these questions, as time and interest allow:

- If you were forced to choose just one Christmas tradition, religious or nonreligious, to observe for the rest of your Christmases, what tradition would you choose, and why?
- What is one Christmas tradition, religious or nonreligious, you wouldn't mind never observing again, and why?
- What is a Christmas tradition you and your family observe in a unique way?

- What stories does your family tell of how members from its different generations have celebrated Christmas differently?
- Did or does your family make Santa Claus a part of your Christmas traditions? Why or why not?
- What do you think will be your strongest memory from this year's Advent or Christmas celebrations? Why?
- Do you attend Christmas Day worship services when your congregation holds them? Why or why not?

Thank participants for having joined this Advent "pilgrimage." Tell them that in this final session together, your group will visit two final "thin places"—"the most spectacular and intimately familiar"—guided by "the very One for whom we have been seeking."

Optional: Light the four purple, blue, or pink candles and the center white Christ candle of the Advent wreath.

OPENING PRAYER

Lord Jesus Christ, our light and life, we praise and thank you for the pilgrimage you made into this world God loves, to make your home among us, as one of us. We praise you for remaining with us through your Spirit as we continue our pilgrimage through this world. Though our paths often lead us through darkness, make our steps firm and keep our eyes focused on you, that we may see you in the faces of those around us, that our faces may reveal you to others, and that, when God makes a home among us forever, we may see you face-to-face. Amen.

WATCH SESSION VIDEO

Watch the session 5 video segment together. Discuss:

- Which of Ann's statements most interested, intrigued, surprised, or confused you? Why?
- What questions does this video segment raise for you?

THE NEW JERUSALEM

Recruit three volunteers to read the texts listed below aloud, one after the other. Invite participants, if not reading, to close their eyes and visualize what the texts describe.

- Revelation 21:1-7
- Revelation 21:22-27
- Revelation 22:1-5

After the readings, discuss:

- How would you describe your overall impression of the new Jerusalem?
- Which of John's images of the new Jerusalem is most vivid for you, and why?
- What is present in the new Jerusalem? What is absent? How do these things' presence or absence point to the presence of God with God's people (21:3)?
- When you think about life in God's presence, do you tend to envision it as John does? Why or why not?
- What do you think seeing Jesus face-to-face will be like?
- In John's vision, the new Jerusalem is promised to "those who emerge victorious" (21:7). John wrote Revelation to Christians undergoing and about to undergo persecution, and experiencing pressure to abandon faith. How would his vision have encouraged them? How encouraging do you find it today, and why?
- Notably, the new Jerusalem is not an image of heaven: John says he sees "a new heaven and a new earth" (21:1), and the new Jerusalem descends from heaven (21:2). What ethical implications does the promise of a new heaven and earth have for us as we live on this earth? What dangers come with focusing too much *or* too little on the promise of this new creation?
- What makes John's vision of the new Jerusalem an especially appropriate one to consider in Advent and Christmas?

CHRISTMAS'S ESSENTIAL MESSAGE: GOD IS WITH US

Optional: Display the elaborately illuminated incipit (first few words) of the Gospel of John from the Book of Kells, a manuscript of the four Gospels in Latin created by Celtic monks on the island of Iona circa 800 CE. Invite participants to respond to the illustrated page. What is their overall impression of it? What details about it most attract their attention and why? Who might the figure seated at the top of the page be? What does the extravagant illustration on this page suggest about the text it adorns?

Recruit a volunteer to read aloud John 1:1-5, 14, 16-18. If appropriate, you may want to invite participants to stand as they are able while the text is read, in keeping with an ancient Christian tradition.

Discuss:

- Why do you think John didn't include a story of Jesus's birth in his Gospel as Matthew and Luke did?
- In a sense, the Prologue of John's Gospel (1:1-18) tells John's Christmas story. Who is this story's protagonist? What is their goal? What conflicts do they encounter and overcome?
- How and why does the story John tells echo the story of creation in Genesis 1?
- What is the relationship between the Word, life, and light in this story?
- How do people, including Christians, fail to recognize and welcome the light today?
- What distinguishes "God's children" (verse 12) from children of human parents?
- "The Word became flesh and made his home among us" (verse 14). How does or should this claim shape the way we treat our own and others' flesh?
- How is the claim of 1:14 like and unlike the prophecy of Emmanuel that Matthew cited (Matthew 1:23)? How is it like and unlike the promise for the future in Revelation 21:3?

- Read Colossians 1:15-20; Philippians 2:5-11; Hebrews 1:1-4; and 1 John 1-5. How are these Scriptures' claims like and unlike the claims made in John's Prologue?

- Ann and Andy write, "Christmas reminds us that God has responded to all ... signs of darkness through Emmanuel." When and how have you seen God's light shining in and not overcome by the darkness?

- "Human beings cannot bring the world healing," state Ann and Andy. "Ultimately, we are unable to fix any of the most profound problems we face." Why, then, do Christians generally attempt to fix and to heal? How can and does the truth proclaimed in John's Prologue inspire, sustain, and strengthen us as we face personal and social darkness?

- "The Incarnation"—the Word becoming flesh—"reminds us that grace is not just a generic word about love but a living person." Although Christians proclaim the Word's incarnation was unique, how is it also a model for us as we love other people?

YOUR LOCAL CONGREGATION

Ann and Andy call any given local congregation, as familiar as it is to those who worship here, "another thin place between heaven and earth." Read aloud from *Come, Thou Long Expected Jesus*: "When we gather in our places of worship, ... as we sing carols, read Scripture, and light candles, we have a sense that we have entered the kingdom of God." Discuss:

- Do you agree with Ann and Andy's statement about Christmas worship in your local congregation? Why or why not?

- If your place of worship were a stop on an actual pilgrimage, what would you most want to show and tell pilgrims about it and why?

- What changes, if any, in how your congregation celebrates Advent and Christmas over the years are you aware of?

61

- What are your most powerful memories of worship in your local congregation? Why?
- Ann and Andy write that since Christians have "seen the face of God in the Child born in Bethlehem, we have no need of a physical building" for worship. When, if ever, has the place your congregation gathers been a hindrance rather than a help to living together as God's people? What do you imagine your congregation would be like without a physical building and why?

CLOSING YOUR SESSION

Optional: Display Pieter Bruegel the Elder's *The Census at Bethlehem* and invite participants to respond to it. What do they notice first? How would they characterize its mood? What details most compel their attention and why? Did they overlook Mary and Joseph when they first looked at this painting? How do we know these individuals are Mary and Joseph? Discuss:

- Ann and Andy write, "Watching and waiting for God's gift of the Christ Child or coming King of heaven do not come easily for any of us." Do you agree? Why or why not? What about the Advent and Christmas season, if anything, makes it easy to overlook their true meaning?
- "We must keep Jesus Christ at the center of Christmas," state Ann and Andy. What does this statement mean for you? How, specifically, do you or your congregation keep Jesus at the center of Christmas?
- Ann and Andy also state, "Grace never depends on us. The Incarnate Word is God's gift to those who have eyes to see, hearts that are open, and believe in and welcome him." When, if ever, have you unexpectedly encountered Christ as a gift in the midst of Christmas distractions?

Tell participants your group has reached the end of its Advent pilgrimage, but that our lifelong pilgrimages with God, individually and together, continue. Thank them for their participation in this study and, if you have not already, make plans for your next study together.

CLOSING PRAYER

Close your session by reading the following prayer aloud:

God, we thank you for the opportunity to come together to discuss, learn, and share about the incarnation of our Lord Jesus Christ. Illuminate our hearts and minds to perceive his timeless identity as the Alpha and Omega, the eternal Word of the universe. Be with us also as we celebrate the joyful mystery of Christ's inbreaking into history. And in the midst of all our celebrations and obligations, help us keep at the center of Christmas this event, the moment God fully and truly becomes Emmanuel, God with us.

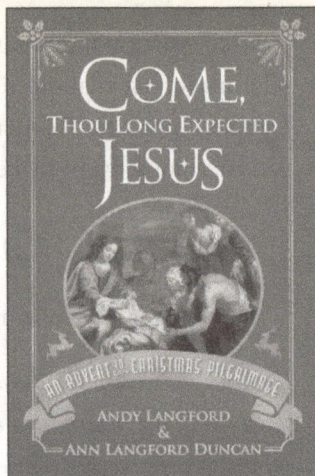